D1413901

It's a Caterpillar!

Elisa Peters

PowerKiDS
press™

New York

For Brodie Patrick Sullivan

Published in 2009 by The Rosen Publishing Group, Inc.
29 East 21st Street, New York, NY 10010

First Edition

Editor: Amelie von Zumbusch
Book Design: Greg Tucker
Photo Researcher: Jessica Gerweck

Photo Credits: All Images by Shutterstock.com.

Library of Congress Cataloging-in-Publication Data

Peters, Elisa.
  It's a caterpillar! / Elisa Peters. — 1st ed.
      p. cm. — (Everyday wonders)
  Includes index.
  ISBN 978-1-4042-4459-7 (library binding)
  1. Caterpillars—Juvenile literature. I. Title.

  QL544.2.P48 2009
  595.78'139—dc22

                                                2007046332

Manufactured in the United States of America

Contents

This bug is a caterpillar.

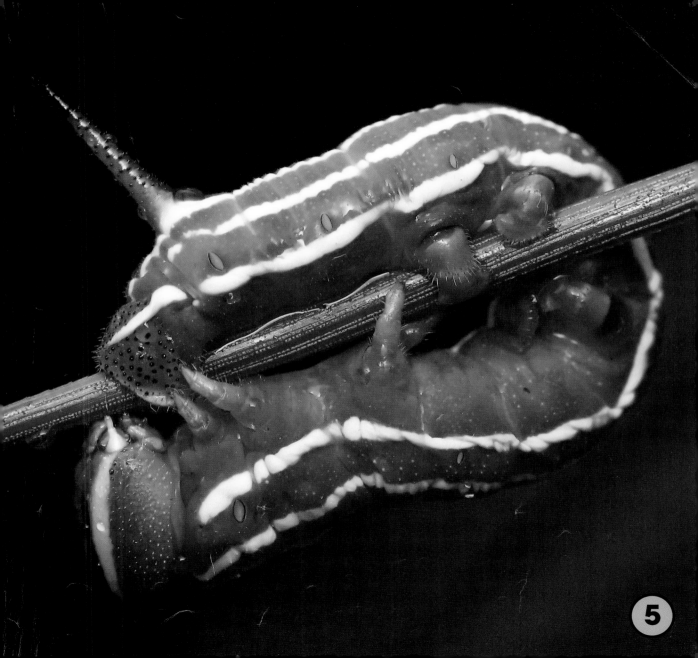

5

Caterpillars have a long,
soft body.

7

Caterpillars come in many different colors.

Some caterpillars have **stripes**.

⑪

Other caterpillars are **hairy**.

There are even caterpillars
with **spikes**!

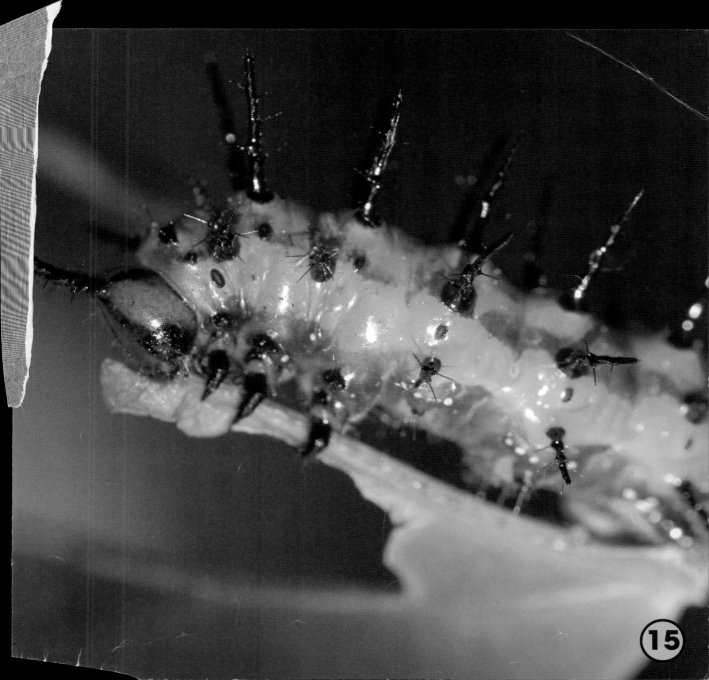

When caterpillars are in danger, they roll up in a ball.

Caterpillars eat leaves. They eat a lot.

In time, a caterpillar becomes a **pupa**.

Finally, the pupa turns into a moth or a butterfly!

23

Words to Know

hairy

pupa

spikes

stripes

Index

Web Sites

Due to the changing nature of Internet links, PowerKids Press has developed an online list of Web sites related to the subject of this book. This site is updated regularly. Please use this link to access the list:
www.powerkidslinks.com/wonder/caterpillar/